YOUNG SIR:

12 PRINCIPLES FOR BECOMING A MAN OFCHARACTER, COMMITMENT, AND COURAGE

LEVI HARRELL

DEDICATION

This book is dedicated to you! Thank you for believing in me. It is my hope
that the words on these pages edify, equip, and empower you to advance in
all areas of your life.

CONTENTS

Foreword

FOREWARD

The road from boyhood to manhood can be extremely challenging. But with the right mentorship and true guidance, as outlined in this book, it's doable. We as a society can guide the next generation. It is our responsibility to not only help them face the challenges of yesteryear, but navigate that terrain with greater knowledge, success and understanding than that of their forefathers.

In this gripping book, Levi Harrell shares a life of both failure and success. He reveals how it felt to develop self-identity issues because he didn't have a father. It's ironic because, while reading this book, I began to see a number of parallels between his journey and my own. I know his story can apply to several hundred thousand people because, according to statistical research, young men who grow up without a father present in their lives are at higher risk of being impacted by many social ills. They're disproportionately affected by violence, drugs, early illicit sexual behavior, psychiatric problems and emotional distress.

That's definitely part of the life story I lived. However, it changed when I moved from Chicago, IL to Atlanta, GA. My life, attitude and choices changed. Then I met my father when I was a man, age 35. I made the conscious decision to leave the past where it belonged and forge forward to form a new relationship with him.

No longer can any statistic describing sons who grow up without their fathers serve as the governing document of my life. The same can be said of every Young Sir who reads and applies the principles of this book. Of course, some young men gain their freedom from debilitating self-doubt through ongoing mentorship and positive influences. Anything that reminds you who you are and whose you are can defeat a negative self image. The process isn't easy. But there is no limit to you becoming the full manifestation of your best self.

It is a testament to author Levi Harrell's strength of character that this book exists. He found his path, then turned around and helped share it with others. It's the embodiment of being a Young Sir – which is what I saw in

Levi when I first met him.

He and his mother joined the church where I served as the Minister of Worship and Arts in 2010. From the beginning, he showed the heart of a servant leader and became a youth and young adult leader. He would schedule meetings with me and always have ideas about how the ministry could grow. He was happy to share his experience and expertise. He often made me chuckle, because he reminded me of myself at that age. Little did I know we had more in common than a love for God and music. Our lives also connected through similar testimonies regarding our family experiences as children.

I always say that the two greatest lessons in life are to first realize who you are. Then second, realize and execute your assignment on the earth.

As you read this book, I am confident each chapter will truly help you grow closer to understanding your specific destiny and purpose. When you finish this book, you will also be able to define success. It won't define you.

I can look back now and see the positive forces that helped bring focus into my life. I remember my great-grandmother telling me, "Don't let your gift take you where your character can't keep you." My high school principal would start every school speech by saying, "You can do it if you just stick to it!" These influences were instrumental in getting me to a point where I knew it was either time to grow up or give up. Most of the young men my age who lived on my block at the time were either selling or using drugs, involved in gangs or incarcerated.

My eventual acceptance of God's plan for my life allowed me to learn there was a different path waiting for me to catch up with it.

I would have benefited from a book like this during those years. Many see where I am, but they don't know my journey to this place. This book is a beacon. It is destined to motivate and inspire males everywhere. *Young Sir* will encourage them to conquer any obstacle and become a version of themselves that will astound everyone.

Young Sir, let this book serve as a road map to your future.

Be You!

Be Great!

Be Unstoppable!

VaShawn Mitchell

Levi Harrell

Preface

I am a 27-year-old man who has seen drastically different versions of what life has to offer.

I've been practically homeless and five years later, honored for my community achievements by one of the highest appointed officials in my state. My father left my mother with two small sons to raise on her own. His decision has affected my entire life. Still, I developed myself into a Young Sir.

WHAT IT MEANS TO BE A YOUNG SIR

The Urban Dictionary says a Young Sir is what cool people call themselves when being modest.
I have a different definition. It's the moment you realize you're no longer a boy but not yet a man. It should be the stage of life when you realize that your life has a purpose, but more often, it's a period of confusion.

A Young Sir is actually living through a series of very pivotal moments where preparation is needed to shape the character of the man he becomes. The road to being a Young Sir can start in grammar school or college. The young men who travel it should have help along the way. But many, like me, really don't. Instead, they have to learn how to reach manhood by themselves. This book is written to show them how to do so, without becoming the type of childlike adult who knows nothing.

We all have struggles.

The problem is most of us choose to do it alone. That means there are few guideposts for others who see our success and want to follow. It is my desire that this book will help young men all over the world live lives of character, commitment and courage.

THE TWELVE PRINCIPLES EVERY YOUNG SIR SHOULD APPLY IN HIS LIFE

There are many excuses why we as men can't make it. But there are also many solutions that can help each of us defy the odds. It is a matter of making choices. I made mine when I developed these twelve core principles and then folded them into the decision-making process of my everyday life.

The twelve principles examined in this book are: Awareness, Purpose, Wisdom, Humility, Obedience, Intuition, Pain, Integrity, Service, Vision, Love and Leadership.

I have been blessed to work with people who are influential, strong and fair. All of them have these principles. I saw them as a guide in my life to get to where I wanted to go. They helped me develop my character because principles are constant.

Principles don't change with the season, someone's agenda or perceptions. Principles remain the same. That's hard to say about almost anything else. The fluidity of 21st-century life makes maturation really hard for boys who want to become good men. Nothing around them stays steady. That's why I see these foundational principles as something each person should internalize.

The Young Sirs reading this book are the next governors, teachers, business owners, entrepreneurs, pastors, fathers and role models. They have to use a mirror of self-realization to move past their own fears or failures. These principles can help them do that.

I know this from personal experience.

ABOUT ME: LEVI HARRELL

In 2009, I lost my job, had my car repossessed, dropped out of school and slept on friends' couches and in a vacated house. I was a disappointing statistic and headed toward being a complete waste of life. I realized that if I wanted to get out of the cycle I was in, I needed to change my perspective. I turned myself around.

How?

Well, I discovered the twelve-step principle program explained in this book. These principles are geared so boys can make the transition to becoming strong men of good character and uncertain young male adults can evolve into decisive male leaders. Both groups are Young Sirs, and I wish them well because in many ways, my journey as a Young Sir is almost complete.

I am now the CEO of a company with my name and the non-profit, LI51: The Empowerment Group. Both help to develop young people. My youth-empowerment company in Atlanta, Georgia helps males ages 13-28 confront self-limiting beliefs. It is designed to set standards that give them the strength to identify the people, places or things that don't support them – and press delete.

As this book goes into its first printing in November 2016, I am on my first CONFRONT (Confidence, Order, Necessity, Fearlessness, Respect, Observation, Negotiation and Tenacity) student-empowerment tour. I visit young people in classrooms all over Atlanta and speak at college campuses, church youth ministries and juvenile detention centers.

In one year, I've reached thousands of young people and watched them confront their fears to reach their dreams. The tour has been so successful that I've created an audio version of my CONFRONT program that can be purchased on Amazon, iTunes and Rhapsody.

However, please don't mistake this list of accomplishments as bragging. This is my second climb up the mountain of success. I was the first person in my immediate family to go to college and get good grades. It went to my head, and I learned the hard way that one decision can change everything.

But the good that came from that low point in my life are the principles in this book. I wrote them to be appropriate in every setting and see them as being the catalyst for stability and success every Young Sir can achieve.

These principles have certainly catapulted me. In 2015, Georgia's Secretary of State recognized me with the 'Outstanding Georgia Citizen' award. Inwardly, I couldn't accept the honor for just myself. I realized that without support, opportunity and the twelve principles described in this book, I would have been just another lost young person who slept in high school classes and carried that same approach into adult life. I've dropped the veil of ignorance and now, through this book, look forward to seeing thousands of Young Sirs do the same in their own lives.

It is my sincere desire that the words held on these pages help you in ways that I will never imagine.

1 THE YOUNG SIR PRINCIPLE OF: PURPOSE

The Purpose Principle:

In all your doing, find purpose in every area of your life. Don't allow life to pass you by and just go through the motions. There is only one you, and it is important to display what you've got! Take pride in finding out who you are. Once you do, you will experience your best life and all it has to offer.

Chapter 1 The Purpose Principle

First, let me use one sentence to explain a single truth about purpose and why it is valuable. We all are one thought away from living the life of our dreams or one thought away from losing it all.

What Does Purpose Do?

Identifying your purpose is important because it gives you the power to shape the world around you. When you have a clear understanding of your purpose, it will allow you to determine the things you study, the people you connect with, where you dwell, how you speak, how you look, and how you present yourself to the world. The foundational tool of becoming a Young Sir with character is joined to the journey of becoming a man of purpose. When you know your purpose it shows. People will tell you that you stand out from the crowd. There is this 'thing' about you that's attractive but can't be described. In the music industry, this is called the 'IT' factor. This factor can never really be packaged or taught. It's there or it's not. But, I believe that any type of IT factor comes from knowing your authentic self and operating in lockstep with your purpose.

Purpose produces motivation.

Motivation provides a catalyst. Because when you have a purpose, you want to know for yourself the reason for anything you do. In other words, motivation is the by-product of reason.

For example, if I know that I have a reason to live, then that will prompt or motivate me to live the best life that I can. That reason provides desire, hunger, interest, and enthusiasm to move forward in purposeful endeavors. A Young Sir needs this because as he pursues life's purpose, he will encounter opposition. It's inevitable, and there is no way around it.

When you find your purpose, some of the people around you will seem to change. You will realize that some once called friends might de-friend you because your goals and theirs no longer line up. People will accuse you of being arrogant and stuck up when the fact is you're focused on things that edify you rather than participating in foolish activities that wind up being a big waste of time.

A Young Sir who is still finding his purpose may mourn the loss of these friends. However, do not allow these 'growing pains' to detour you.

For example, I started two business before I turned 25. They take a lot of my time.

I have had some family and associates accuse me of not communicating or being active in social gatherings the way I used to. I have even had some of my personal relationships end because I was unable to be the man that the person I dated wanted me to be. It is very hard trying to run a business and also maintain relationships with individuals who are not involved in the company. This put me in a very lonely place. But all of the responsibilities for my companies fall back on me. There is no one to blame if anything goes wrong. I am accountable for everything. I love people, but I realized that as I climb the ladder of life, not everyone will grow with me. It was really hard to understand that some of the people who couldn't make that climb included my family. My reputation is very important to me. But I soon began to see that no matter what I do, people who don't 'get it' will always find an issue with me. It took a great deal of self-encouragement to drown out the negative comments that came from those who could not comprehend this journey to greatness. You win some and you lose some. I'm okay with that.

Situations like these aid in the building of your character. A Young Sir determined to find his purpose doesn't run from life's challenges. He embraces them. The more challenges he faces, the stronger he becomes.

Purpose builds confidence. Confidence is the ability to trust yourself. It's a hard skill to develop, because it means you find yourself worthy. I speak on the topic of confidence during my C.O.N.F.R.O.N.T Student Empowerment Tour. C.O.N.F.R.O.N.T stands for Confidence, Order, Necessity, Fearlessness, Respect, Observation, Negotiation and Tenacity. It is confidence meshed with purpose that gives you the ability to go after your goals and aspirations with boldness.

There's something else you should know. Confidence also attracts confidence. It's imperative to exude this so that you can attract it. How do you expect anyone to take you seriously about your life's purpose if you don't take it seriously yourself? But don't get confidence confused with swagger. They're not the same thing. Men with a lot of swagger usually don't have a purpose and can't give you valid reasons for decisions they make.

Therefore, allow the understanding of your purpose to make you confident. Let it make you fearless, certain and courageous. If you have an idea, go after it with courage. If you have a song to sing, sing it with certainty. Whatever you do, do it fearlessly and be confident because you understand your purpose.

How to Identify Purpose

Identifying your purpose can be as simple as identifying the things in life that bring you joy. It's not necessarily what makes you happy, because happiness is temporary. Joy is a lasting heartfelt emotion. Most people find it by identifying the things in life they will do for free. For example, I find joy when I motivate and empower. I do this by way of communication. I have been gifted to communicate effectively. It is my purpose. I do not see dissecting intricate pieces of information and presenting them to others in a form that is easy to comprehend as work. I've learned that good communication is not based solely on what is said but rather what is heard. I make it my duty to obtain confirmed understanding from those I communicate with. When you begin to see positive results come from the things you enjoy doing, you most likely have found something that can motivate your actions for the rest of your life because you have tapped into a well of purpose. It's a very simple thing on the surface. Find what brings joy to you, and simultaneously you can release joy in others.

Joy. Purpose. Reason. These are words that worried me as a child. I stumbled through the first dozen years of life because I had absolutely no direction and couldn't define any of them. I found no reason to identify with any of the things or people around me. This listless lack of purpose meant I had a really hard time in middle school that got worse in high school because I was just drifting. At some subconscious level I knew school work was important, but I only attended classes because I was forced to do so.

However, I could not help but think, "What would happen if I really wanted to be here? What could happen if I knew my reason for being here, my purpose?" Somewhere I guessed there was a bigger picture and if I could see it, then I wouldn't play sick to skip school. Maybe I wouldn't have been slapped with in-school, out-of-school, having-a-bad-attitude-during-school detentions. Maybe I wouldn't have found a way to start or get into fights or stop putting my hoodie over my head and laying my head on the desk to get some sleep. I needed the rest because I'd stayed up all night playing video games. Believe me, I know what it feels like to not have a purpose and the empty activities that can fill your time and mind.

But I also know I could have stopped all the foolishness if I knew – truly knew – why I was going to school.

Instead, peer pressure and the desire to fit in with people who never had my best interests at heart filled my time and life. They would never have gotten a foothold if I had a purpose.

Unfortunately, I never found my purpose in high school. I kept going with the back flow for so long that I fell behind. It became impossible to catch up, so I ultimately dropped out of high school. I never could see the purpose of being there, and even now I feel a twinge of shame with my short-sightedness. It was a really wrong decision and something I usually don't share with a lot of people.

But it was also a strong slap in my face. I began to question myself. I became dissatisfied with just doing something because I could. More and more, I began to ask myself why I was participating in a specific activity.

Then after *why*, I began to ask myself, "What's this going to accomplish?" The answer that came back far too often was one word: "nothing."

So I made it my duty to figure out the *whys* of my life so that I could understand the purpose of my life. This thought process brought me to one of the most important 'why' questions in anyone's life, which was, "Why am I even on earth? Why am I here?" I was seventeen years old when I began seeking the answers to those two questions.

Years later, I found out that "Why am I here?" is the number one question people have all over the world. What I learned through observation is that many young men try to insert employment, scholastic accomplishment, women, families or even organizations and religious groups as their purpose in life. At some point all of these will feel inadequate because they are things grasped from the outside. A purpose starts with what's in your heart and is guided by what's in your head.

A purpose is not static, but it is lifelong. It will take you time to find, but once you do it's yours to keep because no one can take it away.

Becoming a Young Sir of Purpose:

To become a Young Sir of purpose, you must seek out things of meaning. Never allow yourself to partake in senseless efforts. Devote your time, energy, and talents to things that really have an impact. You will always know when impact is taking place by the response you get. It might be the expression on someone's face, their actions in your presence, or even a new-found smile. Whatever the case, let your life be meaningful. Find your self-worth, and let it illuminate every aspect of your life. Let your light shine, and never allow it to go out for anyone. Purpose has no choice but to shine. Be your true self. Then and only then will you be able to help others along the way. Embrace your God-given talent.

MY PERSONAL DEFINITION: "Purpose can be summed up as being the reason for which something or someone exists. It's the place where meaning and understanding come together, producing a uniqueness that can only come from you. Purpose unlocks your identity on the earth. Nobody can give it to you or take it away because it's only released when you accept it. Accept who you are and be the best you possible without apology." – Levi W. Harrell

THE YOUNG SIR PRINCIPLE OF: PURPOSE *Journal*

THE PURPOSE PRINCIPLE

Use these next few pages to begin writing your thoughts and ideas as they relate to purpose. Ask yourself questions such as, "Do I know my Purpose?" If yes or no, explain why.

Levi Harrell

2 THE YOUNG SIR PRINCIPLE OF: VISION

The Vision Principle:

Vision is the ability to see using more than your eyes. It is understanding something beyond your current reality. A Young Sir of vision learns from the past, analyzes the present and changes the future into something that fits his vision. Vision serves as a tool of motivation and inspiration. You will never see the life you can have, if you don't learn how to focus and move in the direction of unseen potential.

Chapter 2 The Vision Principle

There are teachers who knew me as a child who would be very surprised about how I turned out.

I constantly daydreamed. As far back as I can remember, I've always had the ability to see vividly. As a kid, the waking visions were about the toys I wanted to play with or the snacks I wanted the following day. As I got older, I knew the life and career path I wanted. I could see it. But I could also sense the heart desires of the people around me. It protected me in a lot of cases; I always could 'see' when someone was wrong for me.

But it took me a long time to realize that a lot of what I called 'sight' had nothing to do with my eyes.

Think of it like this. You walk into a room and briefly see the door you want to open on the other side. Then all of the lights go out. You use your hands to touch objects that may or may not be there, but it's an inner sense of direction that leads you to your objective. You get where you want to go even though, at the moment, you can't see that it's there.

I call this vision. It could also be described as a spiritual and empathic keenness that can help you navigate through life.

I never fully understood it growing up, but I've always embraced it.

What Does Vision do?

When I became a young man, I wanted to be more disciplined about using this gift. I would constantly try to submit myself to other men because I believed they could train me. But I soon found out that vision does not take the same form in everyone's life. Some of the men I learned from had become excellent in their fields by following instructions. They didn't necessarily have a vision of their own. Some became successful because they learned how to operate as creatures of habit, not men of vision. I became discouraged because I thought I would not be able to find anyone to teach me about vision. I kept looking and found out that the type of training I wanted wasn't taught at my school and barely mentioned in church. Most of the people around me knew little about the topic, because they were zeroed in on trying to maintain the life they had now. They put little or no energy into thinking about what was to come in the future.

Then one day, I looked in the mirror and realized that I had to learn how to develop my vision, myself. I had already taken the first step by accepting responsibility. Anyone with vision has to be willing to take action and be accountable for the results of those actions.

Having vision helped me define myself instead of allowing others to stereotype me. Yes, I was a black male from a poorer neighborhood. That didn't mean I lacked morals. Yes, people put barriers in front of me. That didn't mean I couldn't break them. Yes, there were stigmas. No, I didn't pay attention to them. The ability to write this book came about because I knew I could do it and had 'visualized' its content. I am a public speaker. That started because I had the vision to see how my experiences could help other young people just like me. I am a black man in the United States and with all of the history that comes with that description; I can stand on my own two feet. Again, taking that stand started with the ability to 'see' it; in other words, having vision.

How to Identify Vision

I think there's a misconception about visionaries. They're not just dreamers. Visionaries must also exhibit the strength and fortitude to bring what they see into existence. That makes them doers.

I view vision as a blueprint. If I follow the blueprint of my vision, I can experience my best life. Vision has helped to shape me mentally, spiritually, financially and morally. Vision helps me plan short- and long-term goals. It allows me the opportunity to live beyond the physical restraints that have caused my peers to struggle. I don't see the reality of my day-to-day existence as finality because I also live in the reality of what I see.

This awareness of accountability and taking actionable steps put me on a journey to better understand what it means to have vision. I spent hours studying different pastors, business men, government officials, teachers and all sorts of leaders. I wanted to understand how some of them flourished as visionaries in a world that lacks them. I began to see their commonalities and traits. I began to adopt specific characteristics and put what worked for them into action for me. I never received mentorship or training. No one patted me on the back for my efforts or gave me a pep talk if I made a mistake. I knew in my gut that real visions required accountability to be made actionable. I made it my duty to try and see if what I learned from my personal studies would apply in all aspects of my life. Some did. Some didn't. But I was constantly encouraging myself, because I also knew that real vision requires self-motivation.

Example of Self Motivation and Pay Off

Once I put these findings into practice, I instantly started reaping positive results. I couldn't believe it was actually working. The more I kept going with what I saw, the more confident I became, and the more people began to see me for where I was going rather than where I was in life. I dressed, spoke, and carried myself for the places I wanted to go. But because I understood the accountability factor that is part of having vision, I had researched what those clothes looked like and how my conversation would sound. I spoke and looked as if I were already living in the prosperity of my future. The funny thing is, the more I did that, the more invitations I received to be part of great events and among great people. They saw the me I wanted to be. My vision began to fulfill itself. Make sense?

I believe we are all born with some measure of foresight and vision. But some of you will read these words and either not believe them or not believe that vision can work for you. Well, both statements can be true in your life. But again, your beliefs aren't necessarily your reality. You may not believe that a 40 miles-per-hour speed limit is set high enough for some of the streets that you travel. But you follow those postings nonetheless. What you believe about the speed limit will not prevent you from getting a speeding ticket for driving too fast. Vision can be the same type of experience for you. Daydream about events and goals that you would like to see happen. Give yourself a timetable and a plan of action. When they become reality, try for bigger goals. If they are outside the range of your experience, research them. Then try for what you want. Close your eyes and see it. Now open them and go for it.

It's not impossible. I think we just don't understand how vision works. But the fact of the matter is we spend our whole lives using the gift of vision. As kids, we dream about having that new toy we saw on the TV commercial. When we are teenagers, we envision ourselves walking through our 3rd period class with the brand new Jordan's on and popping our collars because we want to see ourselves as just that cool. As adults, we yearn for the nice, picture-perfect home that we see on these reality shows. The gap in all of these desires comes when there is no plan and no accountability for our actions.

Vision is what keeps me motivated. It allows me to keep reaching for bigger and better goals. The more I see, the more charged up I get to achieve. As Young Sirs we must have a vision for ourselves or else we will get caught up in everyone else's.

This principle described in this chapter can give us hope, strength and security. Learning how to pull what you see in your mind's eye out into reality develops the type of confidence that makes you a Young Sir with Vision.

Becoming a Young Sir of Vision:

To become a Young Sir of Vision you must first embrace and welcome the things you see about yourself inside your head when you close your eyes. Don't allow the uncertainties and the lack of individuality to confine or frustrate you. Oftentimes your vision is just that, <u>your</u> vision. It's your job to research it and figure out how to make it come to pass. It creates a great testimony when you stay the journey and defy the odds. When you have visions make sure you have some way to record them in writing. Put dates and times by them so you can begin to follow the progression of how your ideas have moved out of your head and into real life.

You might also want to make a vision board. This just means you paste pictures and phrases of people and things that you want in your life all in one place. Be creative and detailed so that you can have a clear understanding of the goals you set before yourself. You can start by grabbing pictures of the different leaders you admire. Then take the responsibility of researching their stories. The purpose of doing that is to see what you can adapt from them into your own life. As you begin to take that leap of faith and accomplish one goal, it will stimulate you to keep seeing and reaching for the next goal. Never stop seeing and never stop believing.

Also, when you make your vision board take a photo of it and tag me on Instagram @LeviHarrell or email it to me at <u>iamLevi@LeviHarrellent.com</u> I want to see it!

MY PERSONAL DEFINITION: "Vision is a simultaneous state of anticipation, discernment and understanding. It's a vivid reality that exists in your mind's eye. Vision allows you to walk past the obstacles of the subconscious into a place that is centered and serene. Sometimes what you see is only for the eyes of your soul, until you give it form and bring it to earth". – Levi W. Harrell

THE YOUNG SIR PRINCIPLE OF: VISION Journal

What can you do now that will assist or change the things you see for the years to come?

As mentioned in the chapter, I want you to create a vision board and begin to put all your ideas on paper. Google Vision boards and you will see how to make them. It's really easy and fun. Don't forget to tag me on Instagram or email it to me. I want to see it and make sure you stick to it.

Levi Harrell

3 THE YOUNG SIR PRINCIPLE OF: PAIN

The Pain Principle:

The principle of emotional and psychological pain is simple. It is necessary. Heartbreak and hurt can become the stimulus to ultimate spiritual growth. A Young Sir uses pain to make himself a better man.

Chapter 3 The Pain Principle

No one can escape pain. All of us will get physically hurt at some point in our lives. A papercut or a broken leg will both cause us to experience pain in our bodies. However, psychological or emotional pain can be even more devastating, even though this kind of hurt doesn't leave scars on the flesh. I know more than I care to about this type of pain, because at one time, it ruled my life. But the experiences I've had with pain have given me life lessons. I've learned something invaluable from the emotional pain that used to dominate my thoughts. I want to share those lessons with you.

What Can Pain Help You Achieve?

Few of the people who know me would ever connect my personality with that of a person once tormented by pain. I am an easy-going kind of guy. I make it my duty to find happiness, joy and positivity in all situations I encounter. I think it's safe to say that I live in a psychological place of optimism. Levi Harrell always tries to find the good in the middle of chaotic situations. I smile. I laugh. I do my best to encourage others. It's not an act. I actually feel the upbeat emotions I display. At least, I do now.

However, I haven't always been an optimist. I nurtured that part of my psyche after I understood that even the most joyful people experience pain. I also began to feel differently about emotional pain when I saw it pop up at the most unexpected times. When pain attacked me, I learned to see how it was pivotal in my life. I used it to make myself a better person.

Pain is one of the unique sensations a person can live through because it takes so many forms, and science can't explain most of them. Unexpected deaths, job layoffs, romantic break-ups, sprained ankles, headaches, scrapes, cancer and scratches all cause pain of varying types of intensity and for different lengths of time. What you do with each instance of pain can define your life.

How to make pain a self-development tool

I'm 27. I'm educated and employed. I have great emotional support in my life right now and a bright future. But for years, every time I looked at my face in the mirror, I had a twinge of pain. I tied its imperfections to the fact that my father left when I was child.

Growing up without my father had more of an effect on me than I realized. I have a great mother. There were other male figures in my life, but I always wondered why my father was present in the lives of his other children, but not mine. Did I do something wrong? Was there something he saw that made him leave? How was I supposed to grow into a man without his guidance?

All of these questions plagued my mind during my maturing years. This formed a kind of self-hate, rejection loop inside my head and kept my self-esteem depressed. I felt all of my problems were because of my face. Literally.

You can see the unevenness for yourself in photos. The right side of my face is slightly narrower and darker than the rest. It's noticeable and used to make me feel insecure. How could it not? We are a society based on visuals. We're flooded with images of perfect faces and bodies. Any of us who don't have them are subtly encouraged to stay hidden.

The preoccupation with how we look has caused millions of young people to feel rejected. It's a type of pain that has to be neutralized, because if it isn't, it can ruin or end a person's life.

What made matters worse for me as a child was that I had particular family members who should have provided comfort but instead, added to my pain. I became the centerpiece for all of the jokes. I was called "two-faced," "half-a-face"; you name it, I've heard it.

It wasn't any better in other public situations. I remember there was one incident where I got in trouble for something and I was told, "If you don't change your attitude, I will knock your face straight!"

You don't say these kinds of hurtful things to a young person. All I could think was, "Are you serious?" These were words that came from a person I expected to encourage me.

When you feel that something about you can be attacked and cause you pain at any time, it changes how you feel about yourself. It changes how you interact. As a child, this expectation of pain or embarrassment motivated me to keep to myself. I tried not to deal with people and as a result, I missed out on many opportunities.

Now that I look back at it, I think it's safe to say that my expectations of rejection and pain threw me into a state of depression. It wasn't debilitating, but it did limit my life. I became anti-social. I didn't want to speak to people or make new friends. I expected them to look at my face and reject me. I refused to go to any major school events, parties or church functions.

I loved to sing, but I didn't pursue that talent because it required standing in front of people.

For years of my life, I just couldn't do that because it caused me so much emotional pain.

Can you imagine being young and feeling worthless? I was that guy.

My courage was under attack. My mind and spirit were dragged to absolute lows. I felt as if I had no value.

Here's why my personal destructive loop started. I had received so much mental abuse from others that I internalized it and became my own worst enemy. No one had to say anything hurtful to me because I had developed the ability to attack myself. After a while, it became second nature. Self-defeat was my permanent mindset. I was infected with a destructive strain of pain, and it was going to destroy me unless it got cut out.

Pain, abuse and rejection can feel as real as a broken bone, a pulled tendon or a slapped face.

The type of pain I felt was real. I wasn't the only one. Many young people contemplate or commit suicide because of the exact same feelings.

In 2013, the Centers for Disease Control and Prevention reported that 41,149 people committed suicide in the United States. That means that every 13 minutes, someone is deciding to utilize their personal strength to take their own life. This is also equivalent to 113 people a day. As you can see, this is a major problem. Oftentimes, people turn to the abuse of substances in an effort to heal their inner pain. Some don't realize that it has a snowball effect of bad behavior ultimately ushering them into their very own demise. Nearly ten million adults between the ages of 18 – 25 have admitted to having suicidal thoughts. Almost three million individuals actually outlined a plan to attempt suicide, and half that number actually went through with their attempt of suicide. It has also been reported that men are four times more likely to commit suicide than women. Suicide is ranked as the 7th greatest cause of death for men, while it's the 14th greatest cause for females. The most commonly-used tool for male suicide is firearms. From these stats, it's clear that we as young and old men can be our own worst enemies. Pain is very real, but suicide is not the answer.

I am so glad I get to say suicide is not my story, and my prayer is that as you read my words, it will not be yours. The way to win the battle is to stare it down and fight this very cruel opponent.

In reality, there were twin types of pain for me to conquer. For me, my face and rejection went hand-in-hand. My father's rejection of me and my face also were linked in my heart. They became something I could never resolve. both set me up for a life of failure. But I didn't let it happen like that. I turned my pain into a tool because I had an epiphany. I developed the attitude that if I am dealing with high levels of consistent rejection which cause my pain, it must be for a specific reason. I realized that I had spent my life pushing emotional pain away because I didn't understand its purpose. I decided that if I could find the reason for my emotional pain then I could use it. I took a new approach based on the medical profession.

How to Triumph over Pain

Here's the analogy that explains my thought process. A yearly visit to the doctor usually involves drawing blood, which means the use of a needle that has someone punching through the skin to get to a vein. It hurts, but does so for a reason. Few of us (older than six years old) push this type of pain out of our lives because we know its intent and expected results. We know this is a necessary procedure. Needle pain, at a legitimate physician's office, helps us answer questions about our health. Therefore, we accept this pain because we know it is only for our good.

On another hand, if some random person on the street tried to take that very same needle and stick it in your arm, you'd have a different, probably violent reaction. Why? Because if a stranger sticks your arm with a needle, you have no idea about what will happen to your body afterward. You could be poisoned. You could be drugged. What you know for certain is there is no reason to take the chance. The promise of pain carries no foreseeable benefit.

From my perspective, we treat emotional pain like the threat of a needle prick from a random stranger because we don't see any way it can positively change our lives. We panic or get stuck in our tracks at the first sign of trouble, heartache, embarrassment or rejection.

But here's how I believe a Young Sir should react to painful events in his life. He needs to see that pain is not a stop sign but a pause button. Pain can give him the chance to recalibrate and figure out, not only what has affected him, but why it has done so.

Pain should give you the opportunity to ask questions about what kinds of thoughts and concepts you've allowed inside your head and heart. Pain should make us ask whether these notions are controlling us or have the potential to contaminate us.

I had emotional and psychological pain because I had allowed the negative words, opinions and ideas of others to infect my concept of self, and as a result, I started attacking and limiting myself.

Once I saw how emotional pain had started to control my life, I began to figure out how to deal with it. I had to confront myself head on and take what was meant to hurt me and use it as a catalyst for my own empowerment.

After being depressed, sad and afraid of how other people would look at me, I had to look at myself and say "Levi, get up!" I had to talk to myself daily. I had to face the rejection and learn how to be my own best friend. I taught myself how to applaud and encourage positive things in my life, to fend off the fear of rejection and ridicule.

I stopped letting other people validate me. I learned how to validate myself. I soon realized that the rejected stone made the perfect cornerstone. The pain that used to make me cringe was now merely a light affliction. It didn't go away. It stayed to keep me humble. Now, though, I understand why it exists. Emotional pain helped me learn how to love myself, accept my flaws and use them to my advantage. What I once viewed as a dysfunctional face, I now view as a great conversation piece. It's my chance to share my story and then build relationships with the people who ask about it.

My uneven face has made me a walking, talking symbol of courage and endurance. Now I stand boldly in front of crowds. I speak at functions where thousands of people from all over the world focus their attention on me. I do so with no iota of fear and no concern about my face. Most of my friends tell me they forget its unevenness because it's so irrelevant to who I am as a whole.

Here's how life works, though. There are plastic surgeons who have told me they can perform corrective surgery to make my face even out. I have chosen not to take them up on their offers. My face is my symbol of strength. It is my symbol of triumph. It is my symbol of power. I learned a very important and life-changing lesson about emotional pain because of my face. I learned how to take my personal power back and because of it, I am living the best life I can. Without that life lesson, I might have been a much weaker person. For that reason, I would not change a thing about the pain that has brought me to this point.

It's amazing how pain almost destroyed my confidence, character and self-esteem only to morph into the same tool that produced greater confidence, strong character and self-worth in me. My younger self could have never imagined the man I am today.

Every Young Sir must face painful situations. Emotional and psychological pain hurts. My hope is that you allow it to mature and develop you rather than prevent you from becoming a complete person. Make it your duty to always pause and reevaluate the situations that cause pain in your life. Assess your situation, find a reason for optimism and eliminate the problem when you can. Pain is not a stop signal. It's your sign to push through it and move to the next phase in your life.

THE YOUNG SIR PRINCIPLE OF PAIN

Emotional and psychological pain is life's way of saying, "Hey! It's time to grow, it's time to change, it's time to recalibrate." Pain isn't fair. It does not spare a person because of privilege, wealth or geographical location. Trust me when I say that everyone will experience emotional pain. As a young man on this journey of life, it is in your best interest to begin seeing yourself from an optimistic point of view. This will allow you to handle pain properly and cause you to remain in control. Pain is never something to chase, but if you pause, take a deep breath and look again, you can find a way to make it the catalyst for you to reach your greatest potential. Every up and every down is vital to your growth. Allow pain to become a tool that will let you carve a strong psyche and develop into the Young Sir who will not let it control his life.

MY PERSONAL DEFINITION: "Pain is a mental or emotional suffering most usually caused by external sources. A Young Sir sees pain as a wake-up call that's birthed at the core of great significance. Often times we stop and reject pain, but pain is a chance to take note of the things happening in your life and make necessary changes so that you can effectively keep going. Although I hate pain, I have realized that without it I would remain in certain situations. Pain and affliction have the ability to cause great discomfort, which then prompts the object (you) to make the necessary changes for a better situation." – Levi W. Harrell

THE YOUNG SIR PRINCIPLE OF: PAIN *Journal*

Describe a painful situation that you can utilize for your benefit…

4 THE YOUNG SIR PRINCIPLE OF: LOVE

The Love Principle:

Love is an enthusiastic expression that produces affection. This affection will cause you to affect (to act upon) the things around you, which will then yield an effect (produce results.) Simply put, love not expressed is a love that does not exist. Love held back isn't love at all.

Chapter 4 The Love Principle

You do not love your shoes, new haircut or car. It's not possible. Your heart wasn't meant to lavish that type of affection on those objects and be real; they wouldn't know the difference if you did.

We live in a society that lacks true role models and figures of love. We have made it trivial and silly without thinking about how we learn to love or what knots up inside of us when love goes wrong.

The first object of love in almost everyone's life is a woman – your mother. If you are lucky, as you begin to get a sense of self and are a boy-child, you begin to love your father. On a real innate level that is really an extension of yourself as a man.

I've struggled in this area of expression as a young man because my father left us. My grandfather and my uncle took a father's place in my life. They were great role models and expressed love by their actions. However, they weren't my dad, and I always carried a feeling of guilt. Somewhere I believed I didn't have a dad because of love. He didn't love me and by extension, I didn't love myself.

That doesn't mean I lived a life that lacked love, then or now. My mother loves me, and I regularly see love expressed from women. But I still don't know what it feels like to be loved by my actual father. The objective part of me wonders if his father ever expressed love to him. Nonetheless, I found myself becoming very hard and insensitive because I didn't really know how to express what I'd never seen.

It got to a point that anyone who started showing me love made me uncomfortable. It felt foreign to me. I didn't know how to respond if it was offered. I would become brash about it and try to make the person feel weird, when in all actuality, I was the one with problems. I wasn't the only one though. In my mind, all of these behaviors start and stop with the loss of a father's love. It's something I still don't have and can only dream about.

Can you imagine how many young men would probably never have gone to jail if they had received love from their fathers?

Love is a clear case of actions speaking more loudly than words. When I think of love, I think of forms of adoration or reverence. I'm younger than 30 and have to make a declaration here. I've never been 'in love.' It's also a different emotion than I'm describing in this chapter. There's a level of love with purity that is separate from the heat of sex and the joy of intimacy. The love I want to describe does not change as the love two people may have for each other as mates often does.

The love most men miss having or developing is a fondness or natural dedication to someone. In my eyes, I view it more so as from a parent to a child.

We all know that love can be discussed or dissected from many different angles, but here I would like to explore the way we express it as men. The love I want you to consider in this chapter does not involve sex. While you can't shower it on an inanimate object, you might be able to give it to a puppy or kitten. Love is an expression we as men do not display easily. There's a stigma that's attached to men who show this type of love. Men who can love openly are often unfairly teased as not being 'manly.' Now, I'm not saying a Young Sir needs to be overly sensitive and mushy, but I am suggesting that expressing love is as basic as breathing. You stop breathing, you die. You don't know how to love, you never really live. Men may not come out and say it, but they need to feel and give love.

The Young Sir who learns how to love may first have to learn to love himself and then find how he is most comfortable expressing this feeling. I believe everyone has a love language. For instance, I have a tendency to show love by protecting and providing for people in my life. I want to defend the people I love. I might not always verbally say, "I love you," but my actions scream it.

How To Identify Love

My grandfather knew how to show love, even though I didn't realize it when he was alive. The late Joe Harrell, Sr. probably never told me he loved me, but the funny thing is, he didn't have to. I can honestly say that as I look back over the years, his actions screamed, "I love you" and I am satisfied with that.

I'll never forget one specific 'show of love' incident before I started kindergarten. My mom was trying to drop me off to stay at my grandparents' house. Although I loved them, I didn't want to be there. Everyone knew I was a huge mama's boy (and still am a little bit!) When my Mom put me down, I cried and screamed at the top of my lungs because I wanted to be with her. Instantly, my grandfather came out the room and did his best to comfort me. He pretty much bribed me and promised to take me to McDonald's so I could get a toy. (Clearly, that's all I ever wanted anyway. Who needs food, right?) Nonetheless, this was his way of expressing love. My grandfather always made sure I had food, clothing, shelter, and felt safe whenever I was in his presence.

This wasn't a laughing, joking man. He was very authoritative and didn't show many emotions. But I know he loved me and that he was a great guy. His love is probably the best example of a man's love I've had in my life. It also probably did more to keep me centered than I realized.

However, not all young men get a chance to see that type of love, and I believe some 'get in trouble' as a way to cry out for someone to show it to them. These are young men who will never be Young Sirs, yet still wish someone was there to lead and guide them in the direction they should go. I'm grateful that I've never gotten into serious trouble, but that doesn't mean I didn't cry out, too. In my case, I kept seeking attention from others, when what I really wanted was for my father to love me. I began to have some school issues, self-esteem issues, identity issues, feeling rejected, etc. The lack of love makes you look for affirmation in people and things that don't have the capacity to show love the way a young man needs it. It's the root cause for many young men's personal issues. I believe we as Young Sirs can help to correct this problem by becoming the change we never had. A Young Sir should be able to show love in ways that will make his actions and life beneficial to everyone who meets him.

Honestly, I am still learning how to navigate my way through understanding love in its totality.

You take away the sex, you take away the glitz, you take away the youth and what does love mean?

Part of the question was answered for me in an unexpected way. The first time I felt a natural and instant love for someone was during the birth of my first nephew. Becoming an uncle put me in a position to give what I was not given. My nephew had so much innocence, and it was amazing! I loved that little boy immediately. The emotion almost overwhelmed me. Now, this is how I feel just being an uncle. I look forward to having the opportunity to show love as a father. I might not have had it myself, but I will do my best to let my kids know they are loved.

Honestly, I think it's safe to say that when you strip everything else away - all that is left is love. People with money want love. People with beauty want love. People with power, education, notoriety want love. We all want to be loved. You can be an individual who has absolutely nothing in terms of material possessions, but if you have an abundance of love, you might be one of the happiest people on earth. I believe the person who experiences love is ten times happier than the one who purchases an expensive car to make people look at them in hopes of attracting love.

Inner peace is far greater than exterior items. Now, material things are great, and they aid in the idea of providing or sharing love, but they cannot replace it. I am reminded of the United States holiday of Valentine's Day. We celebrate by buying tons of chocolate, flowers, bears, and diamonds for the loved ones in our lives. But the gifts can't stand on their own. They are only external expressions of the internal feeling.

Becoming a Young Sir of Love:

Becoming a Young Sir of love is to break the stigma of not expressing love. Everyone needs to see, give, or be the recipient of love at some point in life. Your expression of love instantly makes you a change agent who has the ability to unlock closed doors. Be love. Exude love and spread love. Then, watch your life evolve.

MY PERSONAL DEFINITION:

"Love can be described as a fervent regard for someone or something. It's a passionate expression of allegiance and unity. Love shows devotion, friendship, respect, and affection. Now, typically when we hear the word affection we think of it as a mushy embracing term, but I'm referring to affection as it relates to acting upon. Love is an action word so if you have love for someone or something, then action is required. Love is to be freely given, and it produces bountiful rewards." – Levi W. Harrell

THE YOUNG SIR PRINCIPLE OF: LOVE *Journal*

With the next few pages describe your current perspective of love.

How can you better express love to those around you?

Levi Harrell

5 THE YOUNG SIR PRINCIPLE OF: WISDOM

The Wisdom Principle:

The Young Sir of wisdom squeezes knowledge out of every situation he encounters. He acts with good judgement and turns away from ignorance. He's eager to open his mind and heart to insights that the university of life has to offer. He remains a student his entire life, seeks wise counsel and develops a reputation for having common sense and intelligence.

Chapter 5 The Wisdom Principle

I'm woken up. If you don't know what that means, let me put it this way. I'm on a life-long journey to be consciously aware. It started when I realized the importance of wisdom. Actually, it started when I moved from the North to the South. I grew up in a part of Connecticut that allowed me to live a sheltered life for most of my childhood. However, I was mostly clueless about the world around me. I might have remained that way, if my family hadn't moved to Atlanta, Georgia. Man, what a culture shock. Never in my life have I seen so many business owners, homeowners, and people who carried themselves with importance who were African-American, like me. They dressed well, they drove impressive vehicles, owned nice homes and really seemed to have answers. It was intimidating. It seemed everyone was a legitimate mogul.

But the blinders came off as I got older. I started creating the life I wanted for myself and realized there was a dichotomy of duplicity for many 'self-described' success stories. I learned that not everyone who flashed a smile had a reason to laugh. It amazed me that churches and businesses operated without incorporating, which means they were operating illegally. I began to see people make decisions, based on flimsy promises and sketchy opportunities, that could destroy lives. It amazed me to watch intelligent men and women try to claw their way toward a goal that wasn't worth their time. But they didn't know that because they hadn't done their research or appropriate due diligence. These revelations made me choosy about friendships because I found out the hard way that far too many people had hidden motives and agendas.

What is Wisdom?

So, how does anyone learn to separate the fakers from the power players? Here's what I did. I learned to apply one rule to everyone I met. It required understanding a person's motivation for specific actions or decisions. It meant I had to look at them through the eyes of wisdom.

I developed the ability over a period of years. I started using wisdom to assess potential friends.

If a person reached out to me unexpectedly (and perhaps a little too enthusiastically), I started asking myself questions about them. Why were they trying to befriend me? What did they want? Who were they, really? I began to put my surroundings, and the people in it, into context. I watched what people did, as opposed to what they said. It was a completely different approach to life for me and absolutely opposite to the one young Levi had when he lived a clueless life in Connecticut.

The questions I started to ask about the people and organizations around me put me on the road toward developing wisdom and made me a student of life. I reveled in the fact that 21st-century technology gave me a myriad of ways to conduct research. I began watching numerous YouTube videos, reading books and having conversations with older people who knew what it meant to be wise. I opened my eyes to wisdom gathered by people such as my grandmother and church pastors. I learned about discernment and how to weigh whether something was for me or against me. I quickly found it was possible to read the book of someone's life by being observant. They could be age 40, but I could spend a few days with them ingesting information about the path that brought them to a particular point in their lives and learn from their mistakes. I wouldn't have to make them myself. I refused to be the man whose hard head made a soft behind. A wise man doesn't get his butt handed to him for being stupid.

What Does Wisdom Do?

Operating with wisdom saves time, energy, money, emotional drainage, getting stuck in bad business decisions, becoming associated with churches that have poor spiritual foundations, jacked-up personal relationships and all sorts of headaches. A Young Sir with wisdom doesn't make desperate decisions. Wisdom will prevent you from jumping at something without analyzing all the options. Funny thing is, we have been conditioned to think that we don't have options. But that's a lie. You do. Don't allow anyone or any situation to cause you to think that your options are limited to just what's in front of you. When that happens, think twice. It could be a con game or a sign of manipulation. In many, many cases the sooner you realize that, the better off you will be.

In my humble opinion, as a Young Sir, I believe that practicing wisdom is the key that can open many locked doors in your life. True wisdom suggests that you see, hear, and act upon things with a clear understanding and insight beyond what's common to the natural eye. Wisdom's ability to organize and eliminate is given to those who seek as well as embrace it. Wisdom will cause you to experience longevity in your particular career field, rather than experiencing short-term success.

Wisdom has another attribute that most people will miss. It will give you the ability to shut up.

I have noticed that I have become quieter as a result of studying and obtaining deeper levels of true wisdom. I used to always think I had to correct someone or vocalize my thoughts when I heard something that didn't line up with my opinion.

Now, the more I learn, the more I hush. I'm quick to listen rather than open my mouth.

Honestly, at this point unless someone asks me a question or, I watch someone making a seriously bad decision, I don't speak up. I save the knowledge I've accumulated during my short time on earth for those who are ready for it.

Not everyone can learn by watching others fail. Some people have to go through their own cycles of ups and downs. It's like teaching advanced math in kindergarten. There's no reason to show something to someone who can't receive it because they're 'just-not-ready.'

Wisdom requires self-preparation. It rewards those who take the time and make the effort to find it.

When you walk in wisdom you 'know' when it's time to speak and when to stay quiet.

Wisdom will teach you to righteously analyze situations, people, and circumstances for outcomes that are beneficial to you. Discipline and wisdom practiced together will cause you to evolve into something more than a Young Sir. You will become a man who is unstoppable.

Please understand that this chapter can't give you the results from many studies that have been conducted concerning wisdom. There are other books and studies that provide deeper revelations. You might want to search the 'Net and see which ones apply to your life.

I want you to end this chapter with this: wisdom is an ongoing process. You can't teach or learn it in one period of time. My goal here is to provide encouragement that will inspire you. Seek wisdom. If you can attain even a small part of it, you will have one of the greatest treasures in your life.

The Wisdom Principle:

In everything you do, it is important to understand that you cannot effectively make the best decisions without proper knowledge and tutelage. If you want to have truth in every aspect of your life, you must obtain true insight. You must have wisdom. Life without it is too costly.

MY PERSONAL DEFINITION:

"Wisdom is the gift of true knowledge. It's the ability to understand and perceive the correct meaning of a situation or thing properly. Wisdom is obtained in many ways. It can come from life experiences, studies and meditation. Wisdom knows when to move and when to remain still. It's quick to listen but slow to speak. Wisdom is a level of comprehension that only a very few have." – Levi W. Harrell

THE YOUNG SIR PRINCIPLE OF: WISDOM *Journal*

What are your thoughts concerning wisdom?

What are some ways you can pursue wisdom?

Levi Harrell

6 THE YOUNG SIR PRINCIPLE OF: INTEGRITY

The Integrity Principle:

Integrity says, "I will be truthful in public view, as well as in the private." It consistently behaves with justness and honesty. Integrity is vital to maintaining a worthwhile reputation or character.

My Story

Let me be biblical for a few paragraphs and tell you about Jethro. He was Moses' father-in-law after the holder of the Ten Commandments fled Egypt. Jethro is remembered for teaching the tenets of integrity. He is credited with writing the Epistles of wisdom where he explains why a man should want to have the principle of integrity as a guiding force in his life. He taught young men the importance of having integrity while also developing their minds and being truthful.

Jethro wrote that all men of integrity have two defining characteristics. They are men who are both incorruptible and competent.

Incorruptible means the person lives a life of honor, whether anyone watches him or not. It's a trait that is rarer than you might think. I've seen high-profile people who are flat out two-faced. They are gracious in front of a crowd, but can be obnoxious when no one is watching. They have no integrity.

Please understand, no one is expected to dump all of his personal business in the courtroom of public opinion. That's not safe, wise or intelligent. But the issue of integrity becomes more and more important as you gain prominence. A Young Sir with rank and authority will have haters. These are the people who will dig up anything to use against you. Their goal is to look through the closet of your past and find dirty drawers. A man with integrity frustrates them. Integrity means haters can't find what they want, but instead unearth examples that can not be corrupted.

What Integrity Looks Like

A man who can not be corrupted can change the lives of others, just by the way he lives. Let people see what faithfulness, hope and dedication look like when they see you. Then prepare yourself for adversity. Just because you try to live a life filled with integrity, that doesn't mean that you are going to be congratulated. Expect to see just the opposite. Part of having integrity means learning how to display authenticity when you stand in the middle of chaos. Flip the script on them. Show them self-accountability. That is our duty as Young Sirs with integrity.

Jethro also used the word 'competent.' It's a strange unit of language for us to hear in the 21st century. If someone rates your work as competent, it's almost considered an insult.

But that's not the traditional meaning. Competent means we are suitable and correctly qualified. Competent Young Sirs are skilled, knowledgeable and have the trusted support of people who interact with them. You are described as competent if you have gone through all of the proper training and requirements necessary to do the job assigned to you.

Again, competence is displayed less often than I like to see. If you're like me, it's irritating to watch people who have an exalted position but are not qualified (or competent) to hold it. They lack the qualifications and do nothing to hide their inadequacies.

When you read this, it may seem like I'm telling you to follow a lot of rules. If so, you're missing the point. When you start living your life with integrity, you start living a life of freedom. You step away from the strife caused by mess. Mess is unnecessary conflict caused by impure actions, unclear motivations or purposeful confusion. Mess melts around men of integrity. It's hard to blow things up when you have someone who is not posing in charge. Young Sirs of integrity have the potential of diffusing the most volatile scenarios because they lead with an incorruptible personality based on competence and honesty. People without integrity will ultimately fail because you cannot talk about honesty through lying lips.

What are the Effects of Integrity in Your Life?

Men with true integrity have always wielded a great deal of personal power. They are generally among some of the most respected people around. They are also usually versatile. They have the capability to teach, delegate, judge fairly, appoint, manage and either step forward or step back as is needed.

What will it take to become a Young Sir with integrity? A lot.

In addition to being incorruptible and competent, you must strive to be trustworthy and balanced. When is the last time you heard any of those words used to describe somebody? How many trustworthy people do you have in your life? Do you have anyone in your sphere of friends who is both honest and incorruptible? How hard is it to not live your life on tilt and be balanced?

If you spend a minute and just think about the concepts these words represent, you'll see the power given to the Young Sirs who possess them. Those who do, have the foundation of integrity.

Who doesn't want to be around men like that? You'd be surprised. We live in a world that does not promote integrity even though we the people say we want our leaders to walk their talk. However, what it takes to develop and maintain these characteristics appears to be a bit too strenuous for a lot of people.

You have to develop a bold mentality to protect the tenet of integrity in your life. Never allow anyone to attack it. If it happens, nip it in the bud immediately. Don't be a jerk about it, and know that some may not like you for your stance. But they'll get over it if you handle it correctly.

Walking a path of integrity may cause you to lose friends. That's because when you choose to look at incidents through the eyes of a man with integrity, you will begin to hear, feel, and see life from a very different perspective. You will no longer be able to just sit and watch events pass you by. Behaving with integrity at all times can feel like a weight in your life. However, if you crave greatness, it is a weight you should desire.

Men of character, commitment, and courage are usually men of integrity. If you want to join their ranks, prepare to be weary. There are days when you really just want to be like everybody else. But the muscles of your mind can get strong only if tenets of integrity are exercised. Flex the development of a thought process that will react with integrity in every adverse situation. You should strive to get stronger, wiser, and better! It might not feel like it during the initial process, but it will all be worth it.

A Young Sir with demonstrated integrity will find the bonuses of life knocking at his door.

Here are Some Examples.

Corporate jobs are offered only to those who are qualified and trustworthy.

I have been privileged to work with some very elite people and businesses. The majority of the opportunities to do so literally fell into my lap. Most people spend their entire lives trying to be in the company of greatness. I've seen people alter everything about themselves just to be close to a person who holds some degree of fame and fortune.

Well, that is not my story. I'm not a suck-up. Why? Because I truly believe in the value of integrity. I have been offered jobs because of my integrity. Positions have been created for me because of my integrity. It's an important principle in my life. I have been able to travel and speak on platforms that are only allowed for those who have a specific title or office.

People who are famous in their spheres have shared some of their most private and intimate thoughts with me. I'd like to think they have done that because they know I have the integrity to not go and run my mouth about what was shared. I have heard facts about people's families, businesses and finances because they know I am a man of integrity. They know they can trust me. This is an example of character, and I am so glad that my character speaks for myself.

This is not the norm in my home city. I've seen that a lot in Atlanta. People seem willing to do anything to hang on the coattails of someone else.

Atlanta is home to some of the most opportunistic people you will ever find. They will kiss up and even send you gifts in hopes that you will give them an opportunity for which they do not qualify or will help them meet someone famous you know.

Suck-ups suck out. Integrity is a character point that can elevate you in all situations.

Let me describe one more situation where that applies.

The ability to divvy out large sums of money is traditionally reserved for people with integrity.

Have you ever had anyone influential trust you with their money? I have. Again, I attribute the faith in my honesty to the integrity I demonstrated. I've actually run the product tables for certain artists. This means while they performed, I used their phones or computers to make online payments. I handled petty cash, and I treated all transactions as if they were my own. In some cases, I did it without pay. I'm good at juggling multiple tasks and take joy knowing I had the opportunity to make sure they had a few hundred dollars to take home.

I would have never been able to handle money for someone else, if I were not trustworthy. My character spoke for itself and in those moments, I continued to let my actions show the world my level of integrity. To this day, I have great business relationships and some even on a personal level with these people because I handled their business and money as if it were my very own.

There's a long list of opportunities that are never offered to people without demonstrated integrity. Integrity will make you a living symbol of rightfully earned influence now and into the future. A Young Sir of integrity has the ability to affect his current family, his family to come and generations after them because of a commitment to integrity.

In my life, I have received another gift from living a life of integrity; that gift is inner peace. I think it comes from knowing that my integrity is tied to my reputation. In the end, it's really all any of us have. A great name goes a long way, and one that is tarnished can't.

Are there going to be temptations to do things that would cause others to question your integrity? Of course. But create a 'checks and balances system' for your life, and then arm yourself with the most effective way to maintain integrity. Surround yourself with other people who have it. Make your march toward becoming a man of integrity relevant to your life as it is now and how you want it to be in your mind.

Let me add another trait you should add to your arsenal. Men with integrity are noble. I would also like to describe them as unique, not only because they walk in power, but also because they refuse to copy anyone else. A man with integrity is no one to mess with and at the same time also not one who flaunts his convictions. These competent and wise individuals are 'people magnets.' You want to be around them because they are willingly accountable for their actions.

Most of the people I know with these traits (and they are few) are natural leaders. Some are role models and don't even know it. They practice truth at such a high level that 'goodness and grace follows them all the days of their lives. '

Becoming A Young Sir of Integrity:

A Young Sir of Integrity consistently practices the twin behaviors of honesty and truthfulness. He is the same person behind closed doors that people see in public. His actions and words are above reproach.

MY PERSONAL DEFINITION: "*Your integrity is tied to your morality. It is a marker for your ethics, honor and conduct. Integrity is an attribute owned by every noble man. Your reputation sits on the shoulders of integrity. A Young Sir who can be honest and true publicly and privately carries the trait of developing integrity.*"- *Levi W. Harrell*

The Young Sir Principle of: Integrity *Journal*

Who in your life do you know to be integral?

After reading about integrity, what can you do to practice integrity?

What does integrity mean to you?

Levi Harrell

7 THE YOUNG SIR PRINCIPLE OF: HUMILITY

The Humility Principle:

Humility is tied to respect, not weakness. It is a source of strength because it allows you to uplift others. That makes it a strategy as well as a principle. Humility has a way of making you favorable in the eyes of many. It's a formula. Humility yields respect. Respect yields modesty. Modesty yields favor. Humility is part of a universal golden rule: treat others the way you want to be treated.

Chapter 7 The Humility Principle

Men get the wrong idea about humility. Many think the word is tied to being submissive. Of course, in the culture of the United States, that means weakness.

Erase those ideas. Humility is really linked to respect and should be seen as a strategy for life and internal fortitude. It's about your personal posture in public settings. It helps you know where you stand. You know exactly what I mean because you've seen it happen.

When someone enters a room with a lot of attitude or behaving as if he's the top person there, one of three things happen. People test him or distance themselves from him. There's a third action, no one wants. Weaker people circle him to enhance his opinion of himself. But the people he may most want to attract or meet will not be drawn to him or his personal demeanor.

Now let the same person come into the room with a smile and perhaps a kind word for one of the servers. It's a humble entrance that someone of stature may notice. It also gives the person a chance to approach anyone. You spoke to the person with the least status in the room. You were humble. If you speak to the most powerful person next, you don't look arrogant.

Why Humility is Necessary

Now, I don't want to scare you, but I need you to realize that no matter what personal beliefs you have, we are all part spirit. The true essence of humility is like wearing garments of camouflage. It conceals an enormous amount of power so that your enemies can't gauge how to mount an accurate attack. It allows you to hear and be aware of indirect/direct threats. If you exercise humility, you can develop the art of self-protection. However, when it's time to unveil your strengths, your enemies will crumble because they mistook your humility for powerlessness! Humility is a state of mind that allows you the time to plan your path in life.

To look through the eyes of humility is to comprehend what is happening around you. You are able to respond in the most effective way possible, one that will yield a beneficial outcome. We have been programmed to look at life by comparing ourselves to everyone else. But it's really a stupid idea to think that everyone ought to analyze life by the same ruler. You have to judge each situation in your life yourself. It does not make you crazy to think differently; it is actually a force to be reckoned with. You can lose that advantage by not being humble. Never boast, thinking that your idea is the only one. Rest in humility, knowing that your idea is indeed good, but you can enhance it by listening to others.

I am making an effort to stretch your mind beyond the usual thoughts about humility. The principle of humility calls for analytical thinking. You have to apply it to short-term situations to achieve your long-term goals. That's hard to do on days when people irritate the living daylights out of you.

How Humility Looks in Everyday Life

Here's a personal experience I'll share. I'm a public speaker and regularly address crowds of young people. Recently, I had an individual come meet me after a presentation. He then launched into a public and unexpected verbal attack. This man insulted and demeaned my character. He presented himself to me as if his opinion really mattered. He made statements that were supposed to unnerve me. But the principle of humility put the conflict in perspective. In reality, he was a nobody. The only way he would have gained status is if I had reacted to him or given power to his words. Conflict requires two people. I ruled the situation because I refused to let friction develop. Instead, I was humble. I didn't participate because humility allowed me to respond in a way that I would have never done earlier in my life. Don't think for a minute I didn't fantasize about different ways to handle this heckler.

You know, we as men don't like to back down from a fight. In my head, I wanted to let him have it. On the outside, though, I released kindness and smiles.

When he vehemently prodded me for a response, I just shook my head and said, "Thank you for your observation." I did this because I realized nothing I said would register with this man. I could have said, "I have $100,000.00 in a bag that I will give you and a brand new house you can move into today if you retract everything you said." He wouldn't have heard it.

Now, this does not suggest that you let people walk all over you. Instead, learn to choose your battles. Don't win meaningless fights. The one with this particular audience member would not have gained me anything. The principle of humility allowed me to deal with it by letting it go.

I know it sounds crazy, and it will feel weird when you incorporate humility into your decision-making process. After a while, though, you'll see that it saves so much time to just smile and walk away. I understood that the situation with this particular audience member was meant to be a distraction to get me off my game. I understood that my response could have escalated things to a direction that did not create a beneficial result. I understood that the best way to benefit from that moment was to save the story and share it here in this book as an example to show how humility works. I don't have any regrets, and the entire incident has become a teaching tool.

Never allow life or people to get you out of character. That's way too much power to put in the hands of exterior forces. You must remain the captain of your ship and allow the concept of strategic humility to resonate within you. Practice humility. Realize it's a strategy for winning your ultimate goals and objectives. Sometimes you have to be okay with seeming like the lesser man for the sake of getting what you want. Remember who you are and incorporate the attributes of being a Young Sir, and you will be just fine!

Don't allow anyone to make you feel as if walking with humility is a negative trait. Whenever you face opposition, examine the individual who's causing it and see how people respond to them. I guarantee you it's those who practice humility that experience consistent success and longevity in every area of their lives.

Becoming a Young Sir of Humility:

Practice uplifting and encouraging the accomplishments of someone else. Nothing is wrong with receiving compliments but remember to respond with a 'thank you' when you receive one. Let others brag on you. Let your character and work speak for itself. Surround yourself with other successfully humble people, and it will make it easier to adopt this trait because you will see it consistently. Embrace it and watch your status rise!

MY PERSONAL DEFINITION: "Humility is the ability to show respect and modesty in the midst of knowing your own self-worth. It's the intelligence to remove all traits of arrogance from your demeanor without feeling inferior. A humble Young Sir is polite, courteous, modest, respectful, and content. However, he is also confident. A humble Young Sir knows the difference between confidence and being boastful because he can let his work and character speak for him. A humble man lets others brag on him and realizes he is a fool to do it himself." - Levi W. Harrell

THE YOUNG SIR PRINCIPLE OF: HUMILITY Journal

What does the posture of humility mean to you?

How can you begin to practice humility in your life?

Levi Harrell

8 THE YOUNG SIR PRINCIPLE OF: SERVICE

The Service Principle:

The servant principle affects more than you or your personal desires. Servanthood allows your life to demonstrate the law of sowing and reaping. When you sow service, as a selfless worker, you may find yourself reaping it at the level of a leader. Takers never receive because they rarely learn how to serve.

Chapter 8: The Service Principle

Let's demystify service. It is training for leadership. It prepares you by understanding how things operate beneath the surface. It also develops your heart. I've always had a desire to help others. I have learned that volunteering is one of the greatest opportunities to aid in the goals of other people. I feel joy and accomplishment when I am able to put what I want aside and help someone else.

What is Service?

Close your eyes for a moment. Now imagine if everyone spent at least one day a week doing something to help someone else without expecting anything in return. That's service. We all need a push from time to time. Everyday life can burn us out. One form of serving is being the person to come along and help rekindle the flame that makes someone want to get up and go at it again.

Serving is also a great teacher. When people with extraordinary skills or experience take the time to share their knowledge through service, people like you and me benefit. Serving has taught me how to be a leader, and the most important thing I've learned about leading? Serving. Because a leader is a servant who simply stands in front.

The ability to be a man of high rank but yet serve is what truly makes you a Young Sir of character, commitment and dependability.

I want to take this opportunity to share how a servant thinks from the perspective of someone else.

The following description is written by a military veteran. It touched me, as I hope it will you. But more importantly, it made me strive harder to reach a level of serving that can transcend my external circumstances.

What Service Looks Like

The Servant's Heart: from the perspective of a United States military veteran

I learned the true meaning of having the heart of a servant by spending eight years in the United States Navy. As a sailor, the first thing I learned was that I served the people of the United States of America. That meant that I was putting my life on the line for people who might not like me if they met me or who could be racist. I served people who didn't understand why I was serving them. I served people who didn't agree with how I chose to serve or didn't like the idea of military service. It didn't matter what or how these people felt about my service. I still made the choice to do it with pride and to put my life on the line for the very people who might be antagonistic towards me. Serving taught me to be selfless. I learned to put my feelings on the shelf. My service wasn't about me. It was about a cause much greater than anything that concerned me. My service was about the freedom, justice and liberty of those whom I served.

When I left the Navy, I again found value in having the heart of a servant. I understood how to serve people without looking for anything in return. You can't have the heart of a servant while constantly worrying about what you'll get out of it. Instead, you have to learn to be content with the reward of knowing that you just helped someone sleep better at night, that you've helped someone go to college or pay their bills. You offer the gift of service even if the people you serve never say thank you or mention your name.

You develop the heart of a servant when you can die to yourself and run boldly towards what others would run from.

You also learn that as you excel in rank, the more of a servant you become. As you climb the corporate ladder, you have an even greater responsibility to serve those under you. You don't become relaxed and expect others to serve you. The best leaders in life are those who understand this principle. True leaders lead by example, and to do this you must maintain the heart of a servant.

The servant's heart is one that serves regardless of how the person he or she is serving feels about them. The servant's heart is one that puts the needs of others above his or her own. A servant does not complain as he or she grows in rank, nor do they seek anything in return for their efforts.

The servant's reward is that of knowing you have done something that made someone's life better because of your selflessness and willingness to serve.

SERVANTHOOD

No matter how high you get in life you must always retain the heart of a servant. No matter how educated you become, how knowledgeable you are, how many high-ranking people you commune with, or how much money you earn in your life, people will only remember you by your ability to serve. We live in a world where most people not only judge you by what you can do for them, but why you did it.

Serving is also a great way to do a reality check. Many of us cocoon ourselves into a certain style of life and lull ourselves into believing that nothing can burst our bubbles. Wise people know nothing is further from the truth, and your actions can have ramifications you never intended. Serving gives you perspective.

I recently had the opportunity to hand out water and food to the homeless in downtown Atlanta. I describe it as an opportunity because it touched my heart.

Their smiles and excitement reminded me that even in what seems to be the worst of situations there is still hope. It also reminded me that I should live in a permanent state of gratefulness. Most of us should. Many are one paycheck away from losing their lifestyles.

I am a firm believer that the reason I remain blessed and all my needs are continually met is because I make it my responsibility to see that the needs of others are met. Of course, I try to care for my family. But I also try to do the same for people who will never have a chance to repay me. Service is most effective when done without a hidden agenda. Service needs to start in your heart. You should serve without any hidden motives or hope for gain. When you serve, do it simply because it is good.

I used to think that on my 25th birthday, I was going to throw the biggest party and celebrate this wonderful milestone. However, when the time came, I decided to do something different. I decided to spend the first part of my milestone giving back to others. I went to a local Atlanta organization to help give book bags to students who couldn't afford them. The group also provided food for them while they were picking up their bags which were loaded with the school supplies. It was a simple thing to do. But it made such a difference. The children, as well as their parents, were so happy to see community members meet their needs.

Don't be surprised when your attempts to serve are met with skepticism. When my assistant and I passed out sandwiches to the homeless, some of the people at first tried to figure out why we were being so nice. So few people give without trying to take that some thought our gesture of service was a joke. They expected to see some strings attached.

I just felt totally blessed from the experience. Yes. It was my day to celebrate. What better way to do it than rejoice in your good fortune by doing for those who can't do for themselves?

No matter how much you do or how busy your schedule gets, make time to serve others. Have it become a regular part of your schedule. Even if you're in a place where you need to be helped, still serve someone else. The best time to serve is when you need it personally. Never shy away from an opportunity to make someone else's life better. Can you imagine what our world would be like if we all took some time to help our fellow man? That world is a possibility. It can start with you becoming a Young Sir who understands and implements the principle of service.

Becoming a Young Sir of Service:

To become a Young Sir of service, you must be able to put the needs of others before your own. A servant tries to see the bigger picture and fit himself into a place that is helpful. A servant tries to make life better for the people around him. He may do that by involving himself with community activities or just helping a neighbor.

A Young Sir understands that donating time, effort and abilities is linked to being a servant. He also knows that a servant mentality can benefit him all the days of his life because as a well-known passage explains, "Give and it shall be given unto you."

MY PERSONAL DEFINITION: *"Service is the ability to be helpful to someone or something such as an organization, church, political event etc. It's an opportunity to bring value and show favor for others. Assistance, usefulness, and kindness are all terms that can be used to describe the act of service." – Levi W. Harrell*

THE YOUNG SIR PRINCIPLE OF: SERVICE *Journal*

What are some ways you can serve in your community? (School, church, soup kitchen, elderly home)

I want you to find some friends/family and create a calendar for you all to consistently serve in your community. Use this space below to outline a game plane. Make it fun!

9 THE YOUNG SIR PRINCIPLE OF: AWARENESS

The Awareness Principle:

If you are aware, you sense the motivations and feelings of the people around you. Awareness allows you to respond with empathy and not just act on your own understanding about a specific situation or event. Someone who is aware is also receptive. Awareness forms a communications loop and brings people into your life who are willing to hear what you have to say. Never get to a place where you are perceived as unreachable. People who are not aware often find themselves kept out of the mix. You become forgettable when you are self-centered; being aware of yourself and others prevents that.

Chapter 9 The Awareness Principle

Being aware is a big deal. It starts with knowing your station in life and acting appropriately while you hold that position. It's not about what you think of yourself. It's about being aware of how other people perceive you. Some of the biggest blunders in life can come when we are not aware of how much influence we have.

Cliché alert. I worked as a rent-a-cop type of security guard. I wasn't armed, and

I honestly never felt as if I were truly securing anything. But that's irrelevant! As a security guard, I wore a uniform and had a badge. Those two items gave me immediate respect. No one really knew whether or not I carried weapons. They only knew that I was someone put in a position of stopping property damage and break-ins. I did not have to do much talking. Everyone only had to be aware I was around. In the minds of some of the people I was hired to protect, I probably had access to all sorts of devices. In reality, I had none of those.

All I had were the clothes my employers gave me to wear and some basic training. My point is that I was visible to anyone visiting the property. I made them aware of the fact that I was doing my job. Automatically, I changed the plans some people might have had because they were aware of who I was and why I was there.

As Young Sirs, we are responsible men-in-training. We need to be aware of how we affect others and make those who are important to us comfortable knowing that we are ready to step up when needed. It is very important to be actively visible in the lives of those who matter to you.

What Does Awareness Do?

Make no mistake. Real men have a natural authority that generates respect. We are to be examples of strength, support, protection, influence, security, love and guidance. We have to be active participants in our families, communities, government, and humanity at large. You don't learn how to do that in one year and for some males who don't transition into men, never.

If you are a developing Young Sir, awareness means you can never take anything for granted.

Let me share a personal memory that shows what I'm describing. Once, my little brother hid my mom's car keys because he didn't want her to leave the house. Let me set this situation up for you. My mom and little brother are at home looking each other dead in the eye, and he's telling her he doesn't have her keys. I'm in my apartment an hour away from them. But Mom couldn't make any headway so she called me, because for all practical purposes I was the man of the house.

I was aware of my stature in my brother's life, so all I did was have my mom hand the phone to him. He said hello and I said, "Jay, give Mom the keys before you and I have a major problem."

He broke down instantly, asked me to forgive him and gave every excuse in the book for his actions. He just wanted his mom to stay home. I couldn't blame him.

However, what amazed me was that my mother was with him the whole time. Yet, he had the guts to lie to her and not think twice about it. I couldn't do anything more than talk to him. Still he was aware of me as an older brother and the male authority figure in his life. That's the person who made him respond.

The interaction with my little brother was a remarkable moment for me. It was the first time I was really aware of my position in the lives of my family.

To this day, my little brother respects me, and I notice that he does little things to try to make me happy. In his world, I am now aware that I am his father figure. He brings report cards for me to critique and review when I come to visit or just simply wants to be around me and share his thoughts. He talks. I listen. If I wasn't aware of the importance of these chats, I might have blown them off. As a Young Sir you have to be aware of how little things can have a big impact on other people. It might not feel like much, but a hug, a smile, a conversation, or just being visible, goes a very long way. Never overlook the importance of how other people see you.

Knowledge, education, wisdom, and dialog are all great, but they lose their value when you are not around anyone who cares about you. That's why I urge all Young Sirs to become youth leaders and to mentor younger men. However, be prepared to back your talk with your walk. Be a constant example for those who look up to you.

Even though I had no father in my life as a child, I did have strong examples of how good men behaved. My grandfather or uncle could give us a stern look as children trying to play with our toys in church, and we'd put those playthings away immediately. They had made us aware of the authority they carried in our lives, and a simple facial expression could cause us to rethink what we were doing.

Sometimes administering the principle of awareness means you don't have to say anything. You just simply need to be available.

Where to be Aware

Awareness is an integral part of manhood. Being a man requires both knowledge and action at many levels. Men know who they are. Men are aware of the fact that children don't raise themselves. Men love their wives. Men encourage unity. Men get involved with school events. Men instill hope. Men train up other men. Men make a difference.

But men like that don't spring up out of nowhere. They have to learn about themselves, about how to build up others and about the principle of awareness.

We all need men in our lives, our communities and our spheres of influence. If you are serious about incorporating the principles described in this book, then you Young Sir are destined to be the kind of man who can restore order in chaos. Take authority over your jurisdiction and be the change agent in the lives of those who are here now and others who will be aware of your legacy in future generations.

Becoming an Aware Young Sir:

This is an action principle, which requires you to make intentional efforts to be visible in the lives of those around you. If you are a father, you are to be there for your children – not to reinforce your ego but to make them aware of the balance in life. If you are a brother, you are to be there for your siblings. That does not mean you take advantage of their developing personalities, but you make them aware of your own as a model of what they should be. If you are a mentor in any form, you are to make your mentees aware that you will move to the position of manhood, and they are to take your place. Make deliberate decisions to incorporate yourself into the lives of those who look up to you. It might not seem like much, but awareness is one of the most important principles you can learn. When you are aware, even a 5-minute conversation matters.

PERSONAL DEFINITION:

"Being aware is a state of consistent availability and active listening. An aware Young Sir exists in the lives of those who need him. You are aware if you remain reachable, accessible, and ready at all times." – Levi W. Harrell

THE YOUNG SIR PRINCIPLE OF: AWARENESS
Journal

What are your thoughts concerning this principle?

How has awareness changed your life? Or how has the lack of awareness changed your life?

Who do you model yourself after?

Levi Harrell

10 THE YOUNG SIR PRINCIPLE OF: INTUTION

The Intuition Principle:

Intuition isn't just a hunch or a gut reaction. Officially, intuition is the ability to understand something immediately – even when you can't find a conscious reason for it. When a Young Sir begins to groom his inner self, the power of his intuition becomes an incredible barometer and guide. It's important to acknowledge the fact that intuition exists. Those who don't can spend a life fighting the fruits of righteousness and lose battles by trying to make rational decisions in an irrational world.

Chapter 10: The Intuition Principle

Intuition is not fictitious. It's a factor in your life, and it's a factor in your decision-making process, even when you don't know it. Scientists at the University of Iowa and the Medical Research Council in the UK think it's so important that they've started developing clinical trials to measure it. That may not be possible because I believe that intuition has a spiritual basis. It's the inner voice that lets you know when you're making correct choices.

Have you ever been in a situation where everyone around you wanted to be a part of a huge crowd? You might have been fueled by the need to be accepted, but yet you knew deep inside there was more to life than following everyone else. Many of us try to fit in because we think it's the right thing to do. I tried to do that in high school. But I wasn't raised to act like everyone else. When I moved to the South from the Northeast, I stuck out because I didn't have a Southern accent. People told me I sounded 'proper' when I spoke. I couldn't get as excited about the latest trends. Still, for a brief moment I tried to keep up. At one point, I begged my mom to buy me expensive stuff before the school year started. But my goal was to impress people who didn't matter in the greater scheme of things. The only thing I ever gained from trying to fit in was a headache.

Once I finally decided to ignore the demands of peer pressure and follow my inner search for something better, I began to gain confidence and acceptance for a very important person in my life. Me.

Something else started to happen. I started to attract like-minded people. These were individuals who knew how to think independently and were developing the ability to think critically.

How to Identify Intuition

Years later, I found out that the peers I tried to mimic in school were either dead, in jail, on drugs, drop-outs, or struggling to make ends meet. These people had followed external direction for their lives. But there was no reason for anyone to fail. We lived in the suburbs! Many of my classmates had nice houses and great families.

However, those who didn't want to get an education were also following a hive mind. Their life-guide was the external peer pressure that comes from mediocrity. I'm sure many of these young people had the same internal intuition that I did, which nudged them to do something better with their lives. Instead, I saw them try to act as if they were thugs, rappers, drug dealers or some member of a lesser-privileged group in society. There was no need for them, or me, to do that.

Instead, I was blessed to examine the principle of intuition and tap into my gut feelings. They steered me toward a path of self-development.

Once I overcame my desire to fit in with the crowd, I focused my energies on expanding the need to be better that called out to me.

The funny thing is, as you begin to obey your inner voice to go after your dreams, goals, and aspirations, the things you want in life will come to you. But there will be periods of adjustment. When you go against the flow of the crowd, people will first call you crazy and try to discourage you. They will tell you, "You can't do that. You don't have enough money." Or I would hear people tell me, "You're out of your mind. You think you're better than everyone else."

Watch what happens when your life starts progressing. The naysayers will view you from a distance but never acknowledge you. They will stalk your Facebook page, look at your Instagram wall and follow you on Twitter. They will never say a word to your face but will continue to clock your every move. Then, something funny will happen.

When they see you start to accomplish your goals, they'll reach out to you for advice. When they do, they'll act as if they have been your best friend all along. When this happens in my life, I smile, wave and just keep moving. A part of me laughs on the inside. Another part of me is thankful to know my inner intuition has helped me become who I am and will continue helping me develop into who I want to be.

It's hard to accept intuition. Most of us don't like following what we can't see. The spiritually-inclined among us know that's the definition of faith. It doesn't stop us from wanting blueprints for our paths through life. Guess what? They don't exist. Exterior motivators are like the wind. They come and they go. You'll always have a crowd around when you are successful. However, prepare to be disheartened when you hit the bumps and valleys that are a regular part of living. Chances are you'll weather them alone. It can be painful but also a good time to learn to listen to the inner recesses of your own mind. If you have at least one or two people that ride the waves of life with you, consider yourself blessed. Those are the ones who you want to keep on your team.

Expect to experience conflict when you follow your heart and listen to that still, small voice that might be your intuition speaking to you. That inner push may lobby against something you want to do.

For example, I am a public speaker. My aim is to empower, enlighten, and uplift those I meet.

Therefore, my life has to be an example of the message I teach. I cannot tell you to love your neighbor one day and then show signs of hate for my neighbor the next. That would make me a complete hypocrite and affect my character. A specific person might really tick me off, but I have to make a conscious decision to stay committed to who I am. The inner voice inside me will cringe if I try to act out of character.

Yes, I believe that intuition has a physical component. I also believe that people turn to alcohol and drugs to numb the hidden pain that can come from fighting against the path their intuition tells them to follow. Of course, emotional pain can also come from work, stress, family issues and the like. We all deal with these stressors. They're daily parts of life. Nonetheless, that does not give me permission to abuse controlling substances to overcome the matters of life that anger, frustrate or just plain hurt me. Does that mean no one should ever have a glass of wine or a drink with friends? Well, that's based off of your personal convictions. The key is to not abuse any substance that can wreck my thought process or dull my intuition. I have to display strength and courage by withstanding the trials of life on my own because my purpose calls for it. I cannot act like a maniac, although at times I want to. When life feels tough, I begin to think about the greater picture and seek the inner reassurance that lets me know I'm on the right track. I like to think of it as my intuition talking to me. I look forward to the day when medical research can do more to back up what those who walk in faith already know.

Becoming a Young Sir of Intuition:

Fully operating as a Young Sir with intuition is to follow the inner guidance gauge that will produce a greater you. Trends established by others will not lead you into a place of authenticity. You must remain faithful to the voice you hear on the inside leading you to greatness. Stay the course and remember the benefits that have already come from being attuned to the voice of reason and spiritual fortitude inside of you.

MY PERSONAL DEFINITION: "There's a Greek word called 'hupakou' that means to listen. Listening is not a skill that's touted much in the 21st century. Young men are told to be heard. I suggest that a Young Sir knows how to attentively and actively listen to his own inner voice. As he develops the other principles described, that voice becomes louder and speaks with more authority because it is uniquely his and rooted in conscious righteousness."

– Levi W. Harrell

THE YOUNG SIR PRINCIPLE OF: INTUITION
Journal

Levi Harrell

11 THE YOUNG SIR PRINCIPLE OF: OBEDIENCE

The Obedience Principle

One second of obedience can change your entire life. One second of disobedience can destroy it. Which do you choose? Obedience might not always feel comfortable, but it trains you to think in a manner that will have specific outcomes. When you obey the rules that lead you to make decisions based on honorable intentions, you increase the likelihood of staying out of harm's way. You can either be obedient to that calling or spend a life fighting it.

Chapter 11 The YOUNG SIR PRINCIPLE OF: OBEDIANCE

Obedience is one of the most basic rules of life. You live your life in obedience. If you don't believe me, walk across the street. Chances are you will obey the traffic light to keep from getting run over. Do you drive? I bet you obey speed, lane and road direction laws. How do you get dressed in the morning? Do you wear clothes that some might call fashionable? Whose rules dictated your choices?

If you want to get even more basic, think of this. You obey your body each time you make a trip to the bathroom. There was a time in your life you didn't obey those urges in a manner accepted by society. You were called a baby and expected to grow out of that behavior. Thankfully, most of us do. But you see my point. Obedience is a fact of life. What most folks miss is that it has different levels.

I don't want you to read this chapter with the perspective of seeing obedience from that of a child. We're not describing the type of obedience where your mom or dad had to always tell you what to do. Instead, examine the principle of obedience as the ability to look at the long-term ramifications of your choices. It is submission by strategy.

If you have ever had a chance to sit and talk to a series of people who got locked up, you'd hear one theme over and over. Many would tell you they didn't know that the decisions they made would make their lives turns out so unpleasantly. Many would have more of a plan if they had do-overs.

We live in a society of spontaneity. It's applauded when someone makes a spur-of-the-moment decision, and it works out for them. But that doesn't happen for everybody. In fact, one of the reasons we need to understand the importance of obedience is because we are constantly given the chance to make quick decisions, and most of us are creatures of habit. We do what we're used to doing.

So obedience is programming yourself. You're building a list of guidelines that will help you react in a way that will give you the outcomes you want. Obedience gives you a chance to make the spontaneous decisions you would make – if you had a chance to think them through.

Like I said, we don't always get that opportunity.

When obedience feels tough, I think about the greater picture. So why should you be obedient? Here is a list of possible reasons.

Be obedient because people are depending on you.

Be obedient because you're a man of character.

Be obedient because it produces the best results.

Be obedient because you've already put a lot of effort into developing your life.

Be obedient because you are the one who is supposed to make a difference.

Be obedient because it will always produce authenticity.

Be obedient because you are an example.

Be obedient because you have goals.

Even after you read this list, you probably have a question. What or who do you obey?

That's where you have to start thinking about who you are and who is around you. This is more than knowing what you want to be when you grow up. It's knowing how you want to be described.

From my perspective, there's no way around it. You have to find a way to obey a higher power. I have a faith in God that has grown inside me. It has drawn me to really learn to see what is and isn't good for me. It has also allowed me to interact with people of worth who can do more than guide me. They can tell me what to do.

This is what I mean about levels of obedience. Many young men get a real attitude when it comes to taking orders.   Decision-making in popular culture is about independent thinking and self-guidance. However, I want you to once again consider people who are incarcerated. If you were to ask how many made bad decisions based on their own beliefs, I believe the number would be high. There would also be a high number of people who are locked up because they followed directions given by someone else.

It sounds like conflicting information, but it's not.

You don't have all the answers. You never will, and when you act like you do, you will fail. You can bank on that. At the same time, if you surround yourself with people who have the same empty-headed approach toward life that you do, it simply means you all are running toward failure together. Don't allow yourself to fall into a trap of crowd obedience. It's called a mob mentality. These are people who are in obedience to ignorance. Their lives are filled with chaos, and they spend a lot of time lost in frustration.

How can you avoid being obedient to stupidity? Surround yourself with smart people. Most of them are picky about who they want near them. You might have to earn your way into the inner circles of people who answer to the proper authorities.

Who are those authorities? No one can answer that for you. There are people and levels of spiritual guidance that only you can discern as to being right for you, or not.

Obedience is an act of submission or compliance. The important part for you is to be certain that the greater authority you choose is one that is beneficial to humanity and yourself.

Let's be practical when we talk about this. Obedience is not always fun. It's a form of discipline that no one can teach you. It can be an irritating exercise. When you are obedient to a person, you must learn how they think – without losing yourself. When you are finding the spiritual path of obedience, you have to learn how to tune-in to a presence you can't see. It calls for silence. It calls for concentration, and it calls for an open heart.

But most of all, being obedient calls for a willingness to explore what life can offer when you approach it with a desire to be pure. It is an objective you can never achieve, but oh, what a glorious journey you can have while trying.

What is the number one reason for obedience? It's what you have to do to be true to yourself, and it keeps you connected to others because it's not something you can do on your own.

Becoming a Young Sir of Obedience:

You can only become an obedient Young Sir when you learn who and what to follow. Trends can't help you find yourself. Only obedience can help you through challenging times, because you will know what types of decisions are best for you. Understand that obedience is about finding how to live your life by submitting in a way that can help you become the version of yourself that you most desire. Obey, but only after you learn what it means and whose orders to follow.

MY PERSONAL DEFINITION: "Obedience means behaving in accordance with a general principle or a natural law. A Young Sir develops the ability to submit and obey with discernment. He knows that everyone has rules to follow, and there will always be someone who will give orders in his life. He prepares himself so he can choose who those people will be and what rules control him. "– Levi W. Harrell

THE YOUNG SIR PRINCIPLE OF: OBEDIENCE

Journal

Levi Harrell

Chapter 12 THE YOUNG SIR PRINCIPLE OF:

LEADERSHIP

The Leadership Principle:

It is my opinion that every young man has leadership abilities. Taking charge is a part of our DNA. But there is a right and a wrong way to do it. A Young Sir should lead only if he knows when, where and how to do it. Leadership opportunities exist all around you. Some are in your own household. Others are available at church or school. There are community organizations that need leaders. However, any place you choose to lead will require one thing: that you do it effectively. Remember, someone is always watching, and that person may judge you not only on how you lead, but your attitude while doing it.

Chapter 12 THE YOUNG SIR PRINCIPLE OF: LEADERSHIP

Leaders don't wait for things to happen. They take action, sometimes without training, because they have an innate ability that tells them what to do. Leaders take charge with confidence. They follow intuition as it relates to accomplishing goals.

Men like to lead. Even though it takes more than a desire to do so, most think they can. It is an expected part of our culture. In churches, most pastors are men. The police force is dominated by men, and according to the Bible, "In the beginning Adam was the leader over the Garden of Eden."

But leading is not just about taking charge. It's about serving. Any leader who doesn't also know how to serve is often ineffective.

I believe every young man can be a good leader. However, the first person he must take command of is himself. As a leader you must rein in things that are out of control or broken. When something crashes and falls, you should be willing to get it cleaned up – even if it means finding a broom and doing the sweeping yourself.

The first step any leader must take is to stabilize the situation under his command. You might not be able to do so externally, but you can stabilize yourself. You do that by bringing everything – your emotions, mentality, physicality, finances, health, and relationships – under subjection. You have to understand who you are mentally and make the necessary internal changes to lead others. 'Wild cards' and men who can't control themselves make bad leaders. A police officer who reacts in fear can get innocent people killed. He must subject his emotions to his training to be effective at his job and to be a good leader. Become well acquainted with who you are, where you are and bring everything into proper alignment so that you can lead. If you and a co-worker can't stand the sight of each other, yet you lead him as part of a team, there will be problems if you can't control your feelings about him. You are a bad leader if your position becomes a place to bully someone. A leader has to check the status of all relationships, emotions and even health. You are not going to lead an Olympic swim team at age 60 or if you can't tread water. A good leader knows when to step back.

Once you have developed the ability to command yourself, you can begin to experience the power of control. Control must always be joined with the heart of a servant to govern and properly manage. Power-hungry self love has no place in the life of a good leader. It is very hard for people to follow someone who is double-minded, so it is imperative to be consistent. For example, once you have subdued or gained control over your emotions (specifically in a heated situation) you must practice accountability. Keep a check-and-balance system on yourself.

This is probably a good time to acknowledge that good leaders don't need a lot of praise. Beware of adoration. People will naturally look up to you and follow your every move when they agree with what you are doing. These same folks will grumble and criticize when you make decisions they don't like. You will have people who are waiting for you to fail because they are intimidated by your ability or they are simply just haters. In any event, know two things. You are always in control of you, and you have to remain consistent. Don't give anyone any reason to doubt your abilities. Set a proper standard and maintain it.

As I explained earlier, people will follow you because they are attracted to authentic leaders. As long as your leadership and your leadership style remain authentic, you will have followers.

It is your job to develop, equip, and train them. Some will become leaders in their own right. Some won't. But your objective is to help the next Young Sir who wants to grow his own leadership skills in the proper manner.

Take the principles in this book and teach them to someone else. Don't be stingy. Spread the word so that we can change generations to come, one Young Sir at a time!

Let me show you how the leadership principle can work. Please allow me to use my family to demonstrate my point. That's actually where I saw my first picture of effective male leadership.

It came from my older brother. My mother put him in charge of me when she went to work. I was not allowed to stray away from his side when we went out. This created a dynamic that taught me that he was, in some regards, my leader. As I look back, I understand there were a lot of principles in play that I didn't recognize as a child. When my older brother was near, I felt protected. I came to depend on that feeling. If there was a problem, I subconsciously expected him to fix it. If I feared something or was in danger, his presence evaporated the threat. He made everything okay.

My older brother was my leader and my only constant male figure. I modeled myself after him.

Here's the amazing point. Like me, he grew up without a father, yet he was still able to lead me as if he had received parental training. To this day, I admire my brother and his ability to lead his family as if he had lived with a role model. He is the father of eight, and he makes sure all of his children have everything they need. I think that is beyond amazing. My main point is that he learned how to lead a family without a blueprint. He is my example of leaders who step up and excel when needed.

Oftentimes, most leaders actually don't want to lead. They lead because they are the most qualified or in the best position to do so.

I can vouch for this in my personal life. I love to be the man in the background making sure things function properly. However, while there I tend to notice mistakes. There have been many times I've tried to ignore things that were done wrong and stay hidden. But that's not why I was put in that place to start with. Therefore, I come from behind the scenes to make sure those things in the forefront are functioning properly. By no means am I looking to shine or to be recognized. If I see a problem, I just want to fix it.

I often ask myself this question: "Why would I leave unfinished work for someone else to do when I have the ability to correct the problem myself?" Can you imagine the world we would live in if everyone took it upon themselves to chip in and just get the job done selflessly? Can you imagine how smoothly things would go if we all took responsibility for not just only ourselves but our neighbors, too? True leaders don't have a 'me and mine' mentality. We need to lead people in a way that emphasizes the importance of the community. We need to lead in a way that makes people feel that they are a part of the larger vision. Everyone needs to feel like they matter. A good leader makes that happen. Most of us want to know that our voices are heard and our opinions carry weight. An efficient leader can transmit that feeling without getting bogged down in a gripe-fest.

A Young Sir who is a leader knows how to make the people he leads feel valued.

I assure you that when people find a leader who makes them feel appreciated, they will begin to make others feel valued as well.

Part of the reason our world is the way it is today is because so many people try to do things their own way without thinking of others. Good leaders know how to accept and reject input. They look for the ramifications of their decisions.

All leaders have to learn from somewhere. In some cases, leading means teaching ourselves so that we can teach others. The next generation should be able to build upon the things we accomplish. It's unfair to ask those who come behind us to start all over because we didn't properly manage our lives. We as Young Sirs, and men in general, need to understand the responsibility that comes with authority. Remember that you are the seed carrier. It is up to us to make sure that the people, community, and the world are better because we are around. If that can't be said about you and your life, then you have failed at being a leader.

Becoming a Young Sir of Leadership

To become a Young Sir of leadership you must believe in yourself. Never allow fear and uncertainty to make you feel like you are anything less than a leader. Speak well of yourself and learn to empower yourself along your journey. But know this: the moment you stop learning is the moment you hinder yourself as a leader. Stay relevant. Stay aware and stay positive no matter what comes your way. Being a leader is a privilege. You should always try to lead humbly.

MY PERSONAL DEFINITION "*Leadership is the ability to inspire, and direct others. True leadership is not forced; it creates respect. Leaders don't blame others; instead, they try to find solutions. They respond to all situations in the best way they know. Good leaders understand morality and train others to follow what they teach."* - *Levi W. Harrell*

The Young Sir Principle of: Leadership *Journal*

What are some ways you can lead?

Describe the kind of leader you desire to be.

Levi Harrell

SUMMARY

THE YOUNG SIR PRINCIPLE OF: VIVIFICATION

The vivification Principle:
Vivify means bring to life or animate.

Chapter 13 Vivification

Let me tell you something about each of the principles in this book. As you start to apply them to your life, please understand that no one principle will ever be enough to make you reach the life goals you seek. I urge you to mix and layer them. Add humility to leadership, and you might find yourself described as charismatic. Apply the principle of purpose to painful situations in your life, and you may find yourself developing strength. Join awareness with wisdom or service with love.

Any principle in this book can be enhanced and magnified when paired with another. You will grow when you find yourself able to apply three or four at a time in multiple situations. The ultimate goal for any Young Sir is to walk through life able to implement all twelve principles in the blink of an eye. At that point, you are no longer a Young Sir. You are a man with character.

It is a point I yearned to reach in my own life. In my mind, I thought it was something that would take many, many more years to develop.

Then I got vivified.

I'll tell you what that means after I tell you what happened.

Grammy award-nominated gospel performer VaShawn Mitchell is more than just the person who wrote the foreword for this book. He is a friend, mentor and spiritual brother. He recently took the stage at my home church in Georgia. As I have done many times before, I escorted him to and from the green room. After his musical praise session, I stood outside the green room door while he changed to return to the service. Before he left, he called me into the room and asked me a question that was the partial motivation for this book.

"What are you still doing here?" is the question he asked that made me stand still and look at myself from the outside in.

The accurate answer was that I sang in the choir. I went to work. I graduated and started a business. The short answer was that I lived a nice safe life. His question really asked, "Why are you living a life that benefits no one but yourself?" Of course, I didn't answer. I couldn't. I could only mouth some inane comment about "not being ready" and then escort him back to the sanctuary. But I didn't concentrate on the service the way I normally do. I kept looking at myself from VaShawn's point of view, and I really wasn't pleased with what I saw.

Actually, let me rephrase that. I wasn't pleased with what had happened thus far, but it was like finding a perfectly ripe piece of fruit before it fell to the ground and rotted. That question made me prime for picking.

The next day I was almost depressed. The weight of my own inactivity was so heavy that I called another spiritual family member in California. I described what had happened, and she provided the final piece of information that has helped me move toward the next phase in my life.

"Levi, you've been activated," Jackie told me by phone.

Her words made everything fall into place. It was as if I had trained to run a relay race and the runner before me had just given me the baton. I was instantly excited and ready to go. All of the principles I have written about in this book had matured in me. It was time to put them to use. But how? Which one was I supposed to launch first? Well, the book you're reading is the first product spawned by my new level of inspiration. Now let me tell you a secret about it.

I didn't want to write this book. I did it to be obedient. If I did what I wanted, there are several other topics I want to put into book form. But they're coming later. This is my first book because I felt it was what I was supposed to write at this time, September 2016.

It is with joy I can tell you about the pain of not having a father and how it led me to see the principle of leadership in my older brother. It is with happiness I can tell you about the self-control of humility and the triumph that has come from awareness. It is with awe that I can tell you that although I struggled writing the concept for almost two years, God made a way to put it all together in the form you're reading in less than six weeks. It was the time for these principles to be released to bless the lives of other Young Sirs. I am merely an instrument to help those blessings get passed on.

As this book goes into final edit, I am traveling to Miami, Florida, scheduling speaking engagements all over the country and establishing myself as the man of character I have always wanted to be.

However, it took the external nudge of my brother VaShawn and the diagnosis of my own feelings from my sister Jackie to give me the proper mindset.

I had not hit the ground running because I had become comfortable. I had convinced myself that the season for growth and teaching was going to start at some point in the future. I had lulled myself into believing that I had earned some sort of break from developing my gifts and talent. The fire of expectation had left my life, and VaShawn stuck a match in the smoldering mulch before it was completely extinguished.

Now I'm fired up, or as the title of this closing section says, I'm vivified. The definition of vivify is 'bring to life.' It's also a scary term for anyone who wants to live a life of accomplishment. Most of the time you have to vivify something that is about to wither or die. In my case, the aspirations and dreams were merely put on a back burner. When the heat got turned up, well, things started to happen.

This book is the result of what can happen when you apply the principles of purpose, vision, pain, love, wisdom, integrity, humility, obedience, service, awareness, intuition and leadership simultaneously.

I want you to understand that the path that has been given to me won't be yours. Employ these principles. Then know that whatever road you choose is something that will bring you an immeasurable level of satisfaction and contentment. Life is meant to be lived fully, and the only way to do that is to be the best Young Sir possible. From there, move into the next chapter of your life as a balanced and fully-developed young man.

My prayer is that the words on these pages will help you accomplish your personal life goals and then spread the knowledge you have learned to others. Vivify, Young Sir. Vivify.

ABOUT THE AUTHOR

Connect with Levi Harrell

www.LeviHarrellEnt.com | Facebook: Levi Harrell Enterprises | Instagram: @LeviHarrell | Twitter: @LeviWHarrell
book Levi Harrell for your next event under the booking tab of the website.

Made in the USA
Columbia, SC
30 January 2019